HOW TO COOK
CHILDREN

HOW TO COOK
CHILDREN

a grisly recipe book

Martin Howard & Colin Stimpson

PAVILION

First published in the United Kingdom in 2008 by
Pavilion Books
10 Southcombe Street
London, W14 0RA

An imprint of Anova Books Company Ltd

Commissioning editor: Kate Oldfield
Senior editor: Emily Preece-Morrison
Designer: Georgina Hewitt
Production: Rebekah Cheyne

ISBN 978-1-862057-71-5

A CIP catalogue record for this book is available from the British Library.

10 9 8 7 6 5 4 3 2 1

Reproduction by Mission Productions Ltd., Hong Kong
Printed and bound by Craft Print International Ltd., Singapore

www.anovabooks.com

Contents

A few words from our General Editor

If there's any greater happiness than smelling a small child gently simmering in the pot then I'm sure I don't know what it is, unless of course it's the sound of the oven door clanging shut on another one of the nasty little creatures. Some people think that nothing so foul smelling and nose crinklingly disgusting as a horrid brat could possibly taste good, but cooked with a little know-how they are surprisingly delicious. I've been eating children for sixty years now and the whiff of roasting youngster with just a squeeze of fresh weasel and a little grated Rosemary do make me drool all down the front of me dress. And a fancy French dish like Enfant aux Escargot et Grenouilles, ooozing with slipperty frogs and crunchy snails is enough to make me wee in my drawers, eh hee hee hee.

For this book, I've travelled the world on my broom and motorbike visiting witches in far off parts and if there's one thing I've learned, it's that I don't like none of them. I've never met such a bunch of disgusting old baggages in my whole life and most of them don't even look like proper witches. What's the world coming to when a witch ain't go no warts? I told them all, the Witches' Code is very strict – a plain black dress and pointed hat must be worn at all times and for a familiar you gets the choice of a toad or black cat, like my dear old Tiddles. There must be at least one large wart on your face, though you are allowed a mole instead – so long as it has lots of hair growing out of it. None of them paid any attention, but they will when they find out I've spelled all their hair and teeth to fall out... Bald and toothless, now that's a good look for a witch!

Even though none of the crones in this here book is fit to cackle over my cauldron, some of them ain't all that bad in the kitchen with a nice, ripe, wriggling kiddie. This book will show you that even the stinkiest gutter-reared urchin can be made into a mouth-watering pie or pudding. The important thing to remember is to choose your ingredients with care. Always try and use the tenderest, plumpest little ones whenever you can. I only cook kiddies that I've caught munching one of my gingerbread houses. It costs a fortune in building repairs, but it's worth the work for the extra flavour. If you're not lucky enough to have your own gingerbread house, don't worry – even a stringy teenager can taste alright in a stew if it's tenderised properly first.

The best bit about cooking with children is that every time you light the oven you'll be ridding the world of another one of the pestilential, vile little mites. Can you think of a better reason to sharpen your knives and tuck a napkin in? I can't.

Esmelia Sniff

West Bickering, Surrey,
England

Kate and Sidney Pie

Janie Groviller

Cor blimey, me and Roadkill went bonkers when my best pal Esmo told me she was writing a cookery book for kids. Well, I went bonkers, Roadkill doesn't do much since the accident, but I could tell by the way one of his eyeballs fell out that he was excited. Cooking with children is a subject close to my heart. I'm always trying to get more kids in the kitchen to teach them about making good food. I reckon there's no better way for them to learn than from inside the actual oven, peeking out from underneath a lovely puff pastry lid.

As a much-more-famous-than-Esmelia chef who has written a load of books already, it was great of me to send her a recipe. This one will definitely leave you wanting more of my superb cooking and you'll probably want to read much more about me, too, so why not go out and buy my other books: 'Birthday Suit Baking', 'Salads Undressed', 'No Knickers Gnocchi' or my new bestseller, 'Altogether Janie'.

Ingredients

Your main ingredient will be a pair of kiddies called Kate and Sidney. They should be properly fed with hamburgers, pizza, cakes, crisps, chocolate and fizzy drinks. The stuff they get at school — salads, fruit, fresh vegetables and all that — is disgusting. It makes them go all skinny and wriggly. A nice big, fat, wobbly kid is tastier and much easier to catch. I use a burger on a fishing rod to reel them in. It may take them a while to cover the ground, but they always come eventually.

Dead things scraped up off the road — puréed rat, mashed badger, flat cat, etc. and a large sheet of pastry to top the pie with.

The most important ingredient is a television crew, but it's also useful to have a few newspaper and magazine reporters to hand.

Method

1 First of all you need to take all your clothes off and give them to the wardrobe people. Make sure that the cameras are all pointed at you and then take Kate and Sidney out of the fridge. It is important that you talk nonsense all the time. If you can't think of anything to say, do what I do: poke the ingredients a lot shouting things like 'Lovely,' 'Blooming Amazing,' 'Fantastic' and 'Pukka.'

2 Stuff something in the kiddies' mouths, a big hamburger or something. (The audience won't be able to hear all about you if the ingredients are making a racket.) then plonk them in a large pan. Now smush up all the dead things that you found in the road and smear all over Kate and Little Sidders. The flavours will mingle in the pan and taste Blooming Amazing. Now put a lid on and tie it on with heavy ropes so they can't escape.

3 Put the pan in the oven and let it cook at a slow heat for about five hours. Every so often you can take the lid off and find out if your ingredients are enjoying being on television with a celebrity witch. You can take this opportunity to give them a stir as well.

4 When Kate and Little Sidders are nice and tender take the kids out of the pan, squash them down into two pie dishes, cover with pastry and whack them back in the oven until the pie crust goes golden and crispy and the juices are bubbling out the sides. Bish, Bash, Bosh.

Ingredients

A beautiful, plump and ripe enfant that has been force-fed gateaux until it is bursting. To tell when it is ready, just poke the child with a finger. If it says 'owww' then it is perfect to cook.

A bagful of fresh frogs. I look down at my nose and sniff loudly at people who buy them from the shop. The only frogs worth eating are those that you have hunted yourself.

Another bag full of snails — wet, slimy and oozing with flavour. Just like mama used to pick out of her hair.

Just a little bit of garlic, about three wheelbarrows-full should be enough.

Enfant aux Escargots et Grenouilles

Mad Elaine de la Moustache

Ooh la la, but of course French food is the finest in the world, and I the greatest chef in the whole of the France. I say 'pah' to the other witches in this book and wag my finger at them. Their food is nothing but the runny nose-blowings of stupid old women. Now, I shall show you how a French witch cooks — with art, with style, with frogs! You must have only the finest of ingredients, and no children are superior to the French enfants. The full flavour of the mature Matthau, the delicate Dominique, the tang of a Thierry…It reminds me of a joke we tell: 'I tried to cook a young garçon the other day, but I could not lift him into the pot.' The other witch asks, 'Why so?' Then the first witch replies, 'Because he was a little Hervé.' Ooh la la, it is very amusing is it not?

Naturally, it takes a genius to perfectly create this dish. When you fail remember to be French about it. Throw the dish against the wall sobbing and screaming, and then go and sulk in your room for six weeks.

Method

1 First you must prepare a marinade. Into a big bowl pour ten gallons of red
wine and add garlic, garlic and garlic. When you have completed this put
in some garlic that has itself been marinated in garlic for at least six
months. At this stage, you must stir in just the tiniest pinch of garlic.
Too much or too little and the dish will be ruined.

2 Take your enfant and carefully peel it, making sure to scrape off any bruises
or spots it may have. Plunge it head first into the marinade, cover and leave
for a week until it has soaked up all the wine. You should be able to hear it
singing. When ready to cook, stuff the enfant with garlic and place in a
large pan, then remove to the oven while you make the sauce.

3 The sauce will require your snails and the legs of the frogs. It is kind
of the little froggies to give their legs for the sake of fine dining, so you
must remove as gently as possible. I myself have a tiny operating table where
each frog is put to sleep before surgery and then bandaged and given a small
wheelchair or wooden legs and crutches before being released back into
the wild. Also, I provide tiny armbands for when they go swimming.

4 Into a saucepan pour the snails, two or three handfuls of garlic, the frogs
legs and a bottle of red wine. Over a low heat, stir and stir and stir. If it does
not become nice and thick then blow your nose into it. This does not affect
the flavour much, but will help to make a nice gloopy sauce and watching
people eat it will give you a warm glow of happiness.

5 Pour the sauce over the roasted enfant then scatter on some fresh snails and some crushed garlic. To serve, lean against a wall and ignore any diners in your restaurant. They must be made to wait until you are ready. Eventually, when the dish has gone cold you may bang it down on the table, making sure you spill sauce on the clothes of the diners and walk away making rude gestures with your hands.

Ingredients

For the burgers you will need one child, a good lean one with not too much fat unless you want a great big wobbling butt. Some folks do.

Three large bunions, chopped fine, and some herbs – nettles, poison ivy and suchlike.

For the sauce: one cup of Marionnaise, half a cup of Willy sauce and something for the lumpy bits. Heck, I don't know, rocks maybe.

A young French Guy from France. They've got millions of them over there so they don't miss a few.

You'll also need to buy a big HaG Industries mincing machine. They're quite expensive, but well worth buying. There's a million different recipes you can make with a fresh minced child – Bambino Bolognese, Child Con Carne, Shepherd Pie – and sometimes I like to stuff a little one in just for the fun of it.

Hagboogers with Lumpy Sauce and French Guys

Barfa Stew-Wart

Well howdy folks. Let me introduce y'all to the great taste of rugrat burger. It's a great all-American dish, invented right here in good old Salem, Massachusetts, by my nanny's nanny and handed down just before they hanged her, then burned her at the stake, then dragged her kicking and cursing off to prison. She was a tough old critter was nanny. Hagbooger tastes just great hot off the griddle, juicy and pink inside, with a dollop of my very own special sauce and a side order of fried young French Guys. I do declare.

Nanny also taught me the importance of a well-dressed table, which adds a touch of class on any occasion. For an informal meal such as this I likes a simple arrangement in the middle of the table. A nice big mound of dog poop on a stick makes an attractive centrepiece and also smells right appetizing.

Method

1 Light your barbeque. It should be blazing away nice and hot. Now, this here is the fun bit. Get a tender looking child out of the refridgineratoror, and stuff it head first into the mincer, then keep on turning that handle until all that's left is a big pile of fresh pink mince. I just love to watch those waggling legs get shorter and shorter with every turn. Hot diggety.

2 Take the bunions – they should be large and ripe, hacked off feet that are nice and stinky. Chop them up with the herbs an' mix into the mince. Shape into burgers. Some folk like to make plain round hagburgers, but I make mine looks like old nanny's face. She looks right at home spitting away on the flames.

3 When you've put the patties on the barbeque, nice and neat, just mix up the Marionnaise and Willy sauces with somthing lumpy. Anything you have handy will do – stones, teeth, lumpy bits picked out of sick, it don't matter.

4 Now for the French Guys. They all speak funny, so make sure you have a witches' French phrase book. 'Please jump in the frying pan' translates as 'Get in that dang frying pan you!' Shout, point and clout them round the ear until they understand. Once they're all crispy you can chop them into long, thin, fries.

5 Now there's nothing to do but wait for your burgers to get done. When they're smoking on the outside, but still raw in the middle take them off the barbeque and pour on the sauce. Serve with the chopped up French Guys. Mmmmm, I do declare they are sure enough tasty.

Ingredients

For the sausage you will need two young brats, the more spoiled and demanding the better. The sausages made from children called Wolfgang, Hermann, Anastasia I like to share with other witches, but if I find a little boy called Hans I save those sausages to eat at home. After all you should always keep your Hans to yourself. When eating I sometimes dip in mud, because I like to get my Hans dirty. Ho, ho, I am the funniest witch in the book, ja?

Most important is a HaG Industries big mincing machine (the same as Barfa uses) as well as a sausage maker machine and lots of sausage tubes made from parts of the body so disgusting even I don't like to think about it.

You will also need one very upset cabbage and the wee wee of a little dog to taste.

Bratwurst and Upset Cabbage

Gröanhilde von Wartzhog

Welcome, my little sausages, to the kitchen of Gröanhilde, where today you are joining myself and little dog Wiener the Whiner as we continue in the search for the perfect sausage – the Wünderwurst. In German 'wurst' means 'sausage', and I always say the 'wurst' kind of brat is one that has NOT been made into a sausage. It is a good joke, ja?

Many people are thinking that the sausage is just good for eating, but as I have proved, the sausage has a million other uses, from the ornamental to the mechanical. For instance, I no longer use a broom, but ride around on a great big sausage on wheels made by my company – Big Motorised Wursts, or BMW for short.

For years I tried to create the Wünderwurst, but always I failed. Of course, the basic ingredient must be nasty spoiled brat, but what to put with it? I have tried everything: brat with toad, brat with newt, brat with cat ... Now I have the secret. It will be made from brat with brat.

Method

1 The first thing to do is make your upset cabbage. It is not difficult, they are shy creatures and easy to frighten. I sneak up from behind and then throw myself on it screaming 'Achtung Green Swine'. After Wiener the Whiner does his business on it I poke it with a stick. This makes a very upset cabbage.

2 Now hold Wiener the Whiner over a large saucepan until he does his toilet again and throw in the chopped cabbage. Put the lid on and boil for six hours until the cabbage is furious.

3 While the cabbage is cooking it is time to make the sausages. From your larder take two brats. If one is called Hans grab him by the shirt and move him up and down quickly. It is polite to shake Hans. Now, into the mincer with them and make a big pile with the different brats all mixed up together.

4 It is now time for my favourite part. Attach a revolting sausage tube to one end of the machine and into the other end stuff as much minced brats as you can. Pull the lever and the sausage mix will squirt into the tube, giving you one long sausage. Twist the tube along the length to make many smaller ones. You now have a great big chain of plump and delicious Bratwursts. It takes some people a lot of practice to get this part right, but I have always been very good with my Hans.

5 Fry the sausages and serve on a plate with the cabbage, which by now should be completely mad with rage. It should be the greatest sausage ever tasted!

Leg of Aberdeen Angus with Chloeflower Cheese and Tatties

Morag McNasty

Och, so you want to learn the secrets of my flippin' stove, do you? Well, you'd better make this tasty dinner without mucking it up or I'll flippin' curse you 'til you go flippin' purple then pull your flippin' head off and use it to strain my veggies. The last person to make a flippin' mistake in my kitchen is still deaf in one ear. Their other ear is hanging off the flippin' mantelpiece. Aye, and if you make me very cross I might be inclined to set young Wully the Haggis on you, and Wully doesn't have my flippin' gentle, forgiving nature.

This recipe is a favourite at my restaurant, the Now Wash Your Hands Café, which is in the Glasgow Public Lavatory. If you happen to be passing do come in for a bite. It's very flippin' informal, guests sit on stools and dine off a toilet lid.

Ingredients

You'll be wanting three bairns: Angus, a slip of a lassie called Chloe, and one called Tatiana.

Freshly grated Rosemary. I said fresh mind, none of that flippin' dried stuff, unless you want me to stick my head on you.

Olive oil. The best type is squeezed out of sun-ripened Italian Olives.

A strong cheese with plenty of taste. I pick mine out from between my flippin' toes and make a lump in the fridge. It doesn't take long to get a couple of pounds.

Method

1 First you need to get the leg off your Angus. (You can do this with a flippin' big chopper, but I prefer to have a tug o' war with young Wully the Haggis until it comes away. It helps keep me in training for the Highland Games — this year I'm competing in the Tug o' Dawn.) Remove unwanted shoes and socks, then place Angus's leg in a roasting dish. Rub all over with Olive oil and sprinkle with Rosemary. Season, then place in an oven set to Mark, 5.

2 You want the Tatties light and fluffy on the flippin' inside, golden and crispy on the flippin' outside. Chop a little German girl called Tatiana into 3-inch cubes, boil her for five minutes, strain, then arrange around the leg of Angus.

3 Now for the Chloeflower Cheese. To prepare the fragrant young lassie, chop into bite-size flippin' pieces and pile up in a dish. Get your lump of cheese out the fridge and grate it all over Chloe. Add a teaspoonful of Pippa (you may want a pinch of Meg too — just for fun), and place in the oven with Angus and Tatty. By now, you should be able to smell them roasting.

4 After another half an hour, your Chloeflower Cheese should be browned and bubbling, your Tatties light and crunchy and Angus's leg roasted to flippin' perfection. If they are not, then you've done it flippin' wrong.

5 Serve to diners. Think of a large number — then triple it. This is the figure you'll be wanting to put on their bill.

Ingredients

A girl called Tina. Not too young or she will be flavourless, too old and she will be too stringy. Look for shining eyes and hair.

Boy sauce. You can use supermarket brands, but it is oh so easy to make your own. Just put a little boy in a big liquidizer and press the 'on' switch. It is most comical to watch his little face whizzing around.

For the lice you can use head lice, wood lice etc.; any good quality kind will do. Fresh is better, but your local supermarket should have packets of special dried lice if you cannot find any.

Some perfume to make lice fragrant. I like Spaniel No. 2, for the mouth-watering aroma of dog doings.

To garnish, Pickled Whinger. Any nasty infant who moans too much will do, just slice and pickle in vinegar. It is always good to have a steady supply, as who wants to listen to the demanding, spoiled brats?

Seared Tina in Boy Sauce on a Bed of Fragrant Lice

The Dishonourable Lady Soo-shi

Greetings honoured chef, and welcome to the kitchen of Black Pagoda, which is haunted by the mysterious Lady Origami who folds paper into the shape of paper. All who enter here are doomed to legendary death by potato peeler. Today you are most fortunate for I, the mysterious Soo-shi, who am lovely and delicate as apple blossom, together with small dragon Ping-Pong, who makes the prrrrrrp noises and the very bad smells, present the art of cooking Japanese children. Yum yum.

All young people in Japan are prized by witches for their deliciousness. Best though, is thin slices of little girls called Tina. Presentation is most important in Japanese cooking. The dish should be arranged with great care, so please make sure that all lice are warm and sleeping before serving. If not, they crawl off the plate and ruin the design of the food. Also they are difficult to pick up with chopsticks if too wriggly.

Method

1 First Tina must be prepared in ancient Ceremony of Floating Blossom and Chopping of Small Child. Find peaceful spot close to riverbank with willow trees, tinkling waterfall, and old stone bridges. Tie Tina to the tree with ribbons and float blossom in the water. It's very pretty, like a painting huh? Now bang gong, bow to Tina, take up large cleaver and EEE-YAAAAAH, YAHHHH and YAHHHH! Chop, chop, chop. When finished, have a refreshing cup of tea. You deserve it.

2 Place thin slices of Tina in a bowl of Boy Sauce and leave overnight in the fridge. This will give the dish robust flavour of slugs, snails, and puppy dog tails.

3 Put your steamer over a cauldron of boiling water and pour on lice (about a cup per person). This will make them warm and sleepy. Alive they are most tasty and it is also most delightful to feel them trying to escape through your teeth when you eat them. When lice are ready, spray on perfume and arrange in bowl.

4 Now it is time to cook Tina. Remove from Boy Sauce and pat dry, then fry very quickly on each side so she is golden and crispy on outside, but pink in the middle, like esteemed bogey after a nose bleed. Arrange two or three slices per bowl and garnish with Pickled Whinger.

5 Perform the ancient and delicate ritual of Happy Scoffings of Small Child by putting face in bowl and munch, munch, munch.

Pie-Ella

Consuela del Diablo

You like to cook the Pie-Ella with a little muchacha cha, huh? I, Consuela del Diablo will teach you this, but first, we must dance. Toss the head back, stamp the feet to the rhythm of the guitar, rattle the castanets, and slappa the face. Any face will do. Olé! Now, we make the great Spanish Pie-Ella. Everybody love this recipe; like Consuela it is spicy and hot, and full of surprise. The biggest surprise is that it make you go to the toilet for three whole days after you eat it.

In my kitchen, the cooking always is done to the beat of the music. I take the pan out of the cupboard, cha! I slam it down onto the cooker, ha! I slappa the face of the infant and throw her into the hot pan, Olé! And so it is done. At my restaurant, Cabana Bedwetta, all must stand on the tables and dance. It always end up with people picking food out of the hair, but if anyone complain I slappa the faces and make them fight with my bull, Manuel. Olé!

Ingredients

The main ingredient is senorita Ella with the waves of dark, glossy hair, the big brown eyes and flowers in the hair.

Slimy things from the sea, like the octopus and the starfish and the curly animals that nobody know what they are. Must be fresh, must be still wriggling and trying to bite.

Just a little Saffron. She is best to store hung up by ankles in a cool dry place.

Lice. One handful per person and lots to throw around kitchen.

Method

1 Light oven, stamp the heels and bang the pans together, a cha cha cha! Bring the pan down with a crash. Olé! Pour in fresh squeezed Olive oil while holding the bottle high in the air. It splash, it sizzle, it make kitchen burn. No matter.

2 Twirl Ella round your head and toss into pan. The splash will set whole cooker on fire. Now you dance in the heat of the flame, faster and faster while Ella spit and sizzle. She is done after three verses of 'La Bumba'.

3 Take handfuls of lice and fling at pan while whirling round kitchen. Clap to the beat and shake lice out of hair, singing old Spanish song 'Hey Salmonella'! Grab large jug of wine and, holding high in air, pour into mouth taking care to spill over throat and dress. Wipe mouth with back of hand and throw whatever is left into pan. Bring to boil and allow to simmer for ten minutes.

4 Take Saffron out of larder and grate a little into pan. Just a little, gently, gently.

5 When Pie-Ella is bubbling, you must add sea creatures. Pull octopus off face if necessary, spin and slam each on kitchen table to stun, then throw into pan. Making sure you still swaying to beat, put out flames with fire extinguisher, then hurl it out of window. Pie-Ella is ready when is pouring over sides of pan and sea creatures have stopped trying to escape.

6 To serve, dance into room holding dish high above head and bring down onto table with a large bang, shouting 'Olé'! Then jump on table and dance the wild Flamenco, kicking plates into the air and slapping the faces. Y Viva!

Deepfried Small Fry with Fries

LaTrina Skidmark

Well awwwlrigghhht! Fried Kiddies coated in my own special batter, served up in a family-sized bucket for one. Would I like fries with that? You bet your sweet bippy! Make that two, no thirty-six, orders of large fries and a couple of extra large shakes. Sounds good don't it? You can forget salad. Someone offered me coleslaw once and these days they're eating their 'slaw through a straw. The snails in my underpants just ate it right up, mind. I been filling my knickers with coleslaw and salad ever since.

Right here, I'm going to let you in on my secret recipe. It's so darn tasty you're going to want to eat it all the time, so watch your waistline. Mind, I'm lucky like that, I can eat whatever I want and still keep my figure. Any kind of child works, so get hold of some good 'ole boys, and good 'ole girls.

Ingredients

A whole heap of children, as many as you can manage.
I reckon about six per person is about right.

Herb and Mices. Was a time when Herb was a
common name in these parts, but these days
seems like all the boys are called Jeremy or
Sebastian, so you might have to use one of
them instead. Mice is easy to find though.
My iguana Wink catches them for me.
That lizard sure has one long,
strong tongue.

More fries than you can shake
a can of salt over. You just
cannot have too many fries.
Fries are great.

Method

1 First prepare your special coating. Take your Herb
(or Tarquin or whatever) and a couple of handfuls
of Mices and grind them up into a smooth paste. Add
a little Boy Sauce (see page 13) and season to taste.

2 Now it's time to reveal the special secret ingredient.
You'll find that the mashed up Lesser Spotted Rotten
Bottom Snail adds a spicy flavour and its shell makes the
coating more crunchy. If you need some, I've got plenty.

3 You're going to need quite a crowd of children and
all that gingerbread house stuff is SO two hundred
years ago. I got a house made out of computer games,

trainers, pimple cream, the latest CDs, and hair gel.
My freezer's full to bursting. Once you've got as many
small fry as you can eat stuffed in your larder it's time
to roll up your sleeves and chop them into bite-sized
portions. You can use the traditional method, but
I find the handiest labour-saving appliance in my
kitchen is a big 'ole chainsaw.

4 Dip your small fry parts in the special coating and lower
them carefully into a cauldron full of hot oil. They should
hubble bubble, boil and bubble a bit more. Once they're
golden and crispy serve in a large bucket, with — you
got it — a wheelbarrow full of fries.

Moppet Vindaloo with Paul-oww Rice and Samosas

Kideeta Skingh

Peas be upon you, honoured guest, and welcome to India's most magnificent restaurant, the Poorli Belhi. Here beneath swaying palms and pavilions of silk, the spices of the east are served while diners are entertained by snake charmers, tiger pokers and elephant kickers as well as the Amazing Tariq Bindibendi and his Troop of Scorpion Juggling Monkeys. We also have a man who walks across hot coals and sleeps on a bed of nails. He is not a performer, he just could not pay his bill.

If you like your dishes fiery hot then you have come to the right place. Last week I made a cauldron of Moppet Vindaloo that was so spicy that it set the head of anyone who ate it on fire. I laughed so much that I nearly forgot to steal their wallets.

Ingredients

One little moppet, preferably curly haired and sucking it's thumb. If it is wearing a little frilly cap, so much the better. However, it doesn't really matter what child you use, as after one bite of Moppet Vindaloo you'll never be able to taste anything again.

Lots of hot Pippas and spices of the east, such as cobra venom, gunpowder and hot tarmac with half a bunion. If you like your curry extra spiky try adding some pins.

A little boy called Sam and another called Paul for the side dishes. Both will go a long way so anything that's left over can be put in the freezer and used later.

Method

1 First you will need to make a vindaloo curry paste. Mash up all the fiery spices in a big bowl. It can be difficult to make a cobra give up its venom – try irritating the snake by whirling it around your head and then shout 'catch!' to one of your assistants. After the snake has bitten them you can squeeze the venom out into the bowl.

2 Take your moppet and fry in a big pan with the chopped bunion, then stir in the vindaloo paste and leave to simmer. Meanwhile you can turn your attention to the side dish. The Samosa is made by taking a ripe Sam and having a large, maddened elephant jump up and down on him. You'll find that the trampled mush is perfect to wrap up in a light pastry parcel with just a pinch of spices.

3 Check your moppet vindaloo by stirring it with a metal spoon. If the spoon melts then it is nearly ready and it is now time to make the rice. Nothing could be simpler that Paul-oww rice: add a cupful of rice per person into boiling water and then add a young man called Paul, to flavour. He should be shouting 'owwww' 'owww' all the time, but if not poke him with a stick.

4 To serve, a handsome waiter, such as the Poorli Belhi's Raji Bhaji, should take the dish to the table and then be on hand with a bucket of water. There are three stages to eating Moppet Vindaloo. After the first taste, the face will go purple, then the eyeballs pop out of the head on stalks while a sound in the ears goes 'MWAAAAARRRGHH!' Finally there is the sensation that fire is coming out of the nose, which – of course – it is. At this point the diner will want to plunge their head into a bucket of water. This doesn't help but it is fun to watch.

Ingredients

Traditionally, a little boy called Stuart is called for, but as a rule, if it has two legs and its voice ain't broken, I'll have it in the pot before you can sing a verse of 'When Irish Eyes are Smiling,' or me own version, 'When Irish Eyes are Confiscated by the Police.'

A big bag of bunions. I steal these off old peoples' feet by the silvery moonlight and lead them away to a big sack.

A couple of little diddly dumplings, pale and plump enough so they float on the surface of the Stu and soak up the witch gravy.

To be sure, you'll also be needing a cauldron full to the brim with bog water and a frying pan. And make sure you carry a piggywig under your arm at all times.

Irish Stu with Little Dumplings

Iris O'Rambly

Ah, 'tis here you are in the land of poetry and song, where there's faerie folk a peeping out of every nook and cranny, with a diddly aye and a fiddly follderoll. That's why I always carry my fairy swatter. I hates them glittery little vermin almost as much as children – though if you pull the wings off, they be alright in a cake. Nasty little tinkling fellows that they are, 'tis a great way they have with the stealing of children. Now the faeries, they take the human children by the light of the silvery moon, leaving one of their own infants in its place, and lead the little girl or boy off to dance and play in faerie land forever. But I takes the children by the light of the silvery moon and leave a presentation box of fudge in its place. Then I leads them away to my larder. If I steal a little darling boy, it's as often as ninepence you'll find me and Patrick the Piggywig bubbling up an Irish Stu. With a diddly die Di!

Esmelia says: I don't think much of that Iris O'Rambly at all; she's famous for her experimental cooking, but if you ask me there's nothing 'experi' about it, it's just mental. She's been especially daft in the head ever since she made one of her own eyes into a "toffee apple" as a joke to scare the local children. Of course, now she's lost the second sight, but she's got no-one to blame but herself. Aside from that she does smell a good deal worse than most, what with carrying that pig around, so that's alright, and her Irish Stu tastes like ditch water with lumpy bits floating in it. Yum.

Method

1 Set a fire under your cauldron and bring the water to a brisk
boil. In Ireland we usually burn Pete. He gets nice and hot,
but spits a bit at first — trying to put the fire out I suppose
— so bung his mouth up with a sock if you have to.

2 Fry a sackful of bunions in a great big pan over a slow heat,
taking care to burn them. Ah, but the smell of sizzling bunions
always sets me in the mood for a hot dog, or a cat burger.
While they are getting charred and black and your bog water
coming to the boil, chop Stu up into 1-inch cubes and add to
the cauldron. When your bunions are done stir these in too.

3 Now there's nothing' to do for about six hours while your Stu
bubbles and thickens. Patrick the Piggywig and I like to go to
the pub for the listening to Irish music endurance contest and
to find out what the 'crack' is. Usually it's a long split in the
wall. I don't know why everyone is so interested in it.

4 Right, now 'tis time to add the dumplings to the Stu, so stagger
home from the pub, singing 'a hey diddly, piggy's going to be a
married,' as you go, and dump your dumplings in the pot. After
half an hour, they should be all puffed up and floating face down
in a Stu that's as thick and disgusting as I am. Serve straight
into a large trough and you and your pig can tuck in a napkin
and enjoy a proper Irish treat, with a pidilly widdly pee.

Cajun Cherub Gumbo

Maman Bumbumbaya

This here Gumbo is full of fun magic of a kind I done made up myself. I calls it Doodoo Magic. Now Doodoo is a little bit like old Voodoo, except it smells bad, just like the Gumbo. Them Voodoo folks, they sticks pins in little dollies that's supposed to look like people, but I reckon it's a dang sight more powerful to stick them pins in the actual folks themselves. Ain't a spell in the world as good as someone you've taken a disliking to walking around full of pins. They sure as dang know they're in deep Doodoo.

You can make the Gumbo with any old boy or girl child. Down here in the swamp I can't afford to be fussy. It ain't easy findin' a child, but every now and again the alligators snatches one off the riverbank and I just jump on that 'gator's back and punch it until that varmint lets go...

Ingredients

A cherub. Try and get one that the alligators ain't chewed too much.

Swamp water. You want about ten buckets full, making sure you gets the dark brown ooze as well as the green slimy stuff floating on top.

All kinds of slithering swamp creatures. You should have poisonous whiskery things with hundreds of legs, great big poisonous snakes, poisonous frogs, poisonous clams and whatever else you happen to find that day that looks as though it'd give you one big bellyache.

Laddies' fingers. The ones you want are fresh off little boy children and should have dirty fingernails on the end. Mind you, I have had good results from Ladies' Fingers, too. Just make sure you take the rings off or you might break a tooth.

Method

1 Pour the swamp water into a big cauldron and simmer
for hours, stirring now and then to make sure the ooze
doesn't settle at the bottom. While it's boiling I like
to throw the Baron in with a rock tied to his legs.
He don't mind and it gives the water the subtle flavour
of zombie cockerel.

2 In the meantime, get your wriggling bag of swamp
creatures. Take off all the bits that look nasty to eat —
wings, claws, heads, whiskers, teeth, and all that. These
are the bits you'll be wanting. The rest you can throw out
or feed to the alligators. Make a separate pile of eyeballs.

3 Chuck all the squirmy things into the pot with the Laddies'
Fingers. Now's the time to add the child. I always toss a
couple of snakes in, too. It helps with the flavour, but more
importantly, it's a dang good cackle watching the child
being chased around the pot.

4 Now let the Gumbo bubble gently for about three days. You can lean over it mumbling strange sounding spells and summoning the spirit of Chatanooga Choo Choo if you likes, it's all part of the Doodoo.

5 The Gumbo is done when the leaves on the trees around have gone brown and birds flying overhead start dropping out of the sky. To serve, garnish with eyeballs. You may want to push some of them under so you gets a nice surprise when you finds them staring out of your bowl. Also one or two live frogs or snakes, squirming around on the bottom don't go amiss. And maybe a little cheese grated on top.

Ingredients

One tasty frittongak – which can be tricky to find if you live a thousand miles from the nearest town. Hitch the penguins up to your sleigh and be prepared to cover a lot of ground, keeping your eyes peeled for telltale signs that children are around. Big mounds of snow wearing hats with a carrot for a nose and two coal eyes are a dead giveaway.

A dozen fat penguins and some moss for the sauce.

Snow. Try and get hold of the light, slightly powdery variety rather than the wet, sticky stuff. I find it tastes of pineapple.

You'll also need some foil. It's a busy life being a witch in a frozen wasteland, so if you've run out don't bother making the six month trip to the shops, your Baked Alaskan will just turn out a little bit more crispy. Even so, it'll still be a lot tastier than raw penguin.

54

Baked Alaskan

Dances with Penguins

Brrrrrrrr, it's turned out chilly again. Last week it got so frosty that one of my toes snapped right off. Not that I'm complaining, it made a tasty snack, but I do dislike being freezing cold all the time. In my language there are thirty-six different words for snow and every single one of them means 'horrible pesky stuff.'

If there's one thing I hate more than the cold, it's eating penguins. Breakfast, lunch, and dinner it's Penguin on Toast, Mashed Penguin, or Penguin Surprise (the surprise is it's just a dead penguin on a stick). That's why I cook up my favourite Baked Alaskan whenever I can. It does take a while to peel them, but the sight of a little frittongak — as we call the children up here in the frozen north — shivering in its underwear while the fire gets going is as much fun as teaching penguins to fly by throwing them off cliffs.

Method

1 The first thing to do once you've sighted a frittongak is to prepare it for the long journey back to your igloo. Cut a hole in the ice, sneak up on the little one and push them in. When they bob to the surface of the water in a big block of ice they are ready to take home and will stay fresh for up to 3 months.

2 When you are ready to start cooking you will need to light a fire, which isn't easy when there's just snow and ice as far as the eye can see. I've tried and tried but I just cannot get snow to burn. Luckily though, there are always plenty of penguins around. It can take a while to get a fire going by rubbing two penguins together, but the end result is worth it.

3 Season the frittongak with a few pinches of snow and a tiny squeeze of walrus. Wrap in foil.

4 Throw the foil package on the fire to cook and turn your attention to the sauce. To prepare you will need to hold your penguins upside down and squeeze them until all the fish they've eaten comes out of their little beaks. Mix this in a pan, stir in some moss you've scraped off a stone and warm it on the fire.

5 To serve, pour your sauce over the frittongak and garnish with a spoon of snow. If you're still hungry after then I've found that a dessert of light, fluffy moose goes especially well.

Ingredients

Some shrimps fresh off the beach – they should be wriggly as a bowl of maggots on Christmas morning and pink as a dingo's bum. How many depends on how hungry you are. I can usually manage three, so you want a couple of sacks-full if you have friends.

Suncream, factor 50.

Something to use as a marinade – beer or some kind of cold, frothy, amber beverage will do.

You'll also need some long, pointed sticks to use as skewers and rope to tie the shrimps on with.

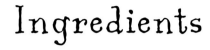

Barbied Shrimps

Shiela Q. Barby

G'day. When the sun's going down under after a hard day surfing and wrestling giant squid, there's nothing me and my jellyfish Bruce like more than munching hot Australian shrimps grilled right on the beach. The way those children sizzle and pop over the coals is fair dinkum and I love the way the juices run down your chin while you're eating them. They're easy to find, too. In this great country there's always loads of them just sitting around making sand castles or paddling in the sea. All you need is a big net. If they're too noisy stun them with a bong on the head. I've got a special stick for this, I call it my Billybonger.

There's nothing better than good food in the open air, so when you're on the beach, always remember: Slip, Slap, Slop – Slip 'em in the net, Slap 'em on the barby, Slop on some tomato ketchup. No worries.

Method

1 Before you set off to catch your shrimps make sure everything is prepared – get your barbeque ready and cut the skewers to length. I've also found it wise to test a few tins of 'marinade' to make sure it's properly cold and tastes right. It's worth taking some time on getting this part right – after all, you can't make a windsurfer out of a wallaby's ear, right?

2 When you've got a nice catch in the net, cover each shrimp in suncream. Not only does it protect the skin from harmful rays, but it helps them crisp up nicely on the grill. Tie a couple of shrimps to each stick and pour on your marinade. About a teaspoon per shrimp is enough.

3 Put the skewers on the grill and relax in the sunshine while you wait for your shrimps to cook, turning occasionally. While you're just sitting there you and your jellyfish might want to dispose of any leftover marinade. I don't mind if I didgeridoo – cheers Bruce!

4 When the shrimps are all charred and burned that's when you know they're ready. Don't bother with all that posh plates and knives and forks stuff – just grab a skewer, lean up against a palm tree, and start chewing. Some witches like to take off the heads, but it's my favourite bit, crunchy on the outside and gooey on the inside.

Apple Betty with Eyes-Cream

Nanny Todd

Oh, I just love children. With their happy smiles and dirty faces; I could just eat them all up. But not before I've given them a bag of sweeties, a Nanny hug, and let them play with my little canary, Killer. It does my soft old heart good to see them having a gay time, running screaming around the garden while Killer tweets and pecks at their heads. When they get tired, I drag them up to the porch for a glass of my special home-made lemonade. After that it's a light bop on the head and into the refrigerator with the little darlings. The only trouble is, I'm such a poor, twittery old lady, I can never decide what to make with them. Unless I'm lucky enough to have a visit from a little girl called Betty. Then, I always make my famous Apple Betty, which goes down such a treat at the Horsewhip town picnic in the summer, even if I do say so myself. Perfect with frosty eyes-cream and scattered with crunchy chopped nits.

Esmelia says Though I'm not saying her cooking ain't passable, Germolina Todd ain't hardly a witch at all. I don't call kindly old ladies who live in pretty cottages and call themselves Nanny, witches. I call them a disgrace. Still, if you have a sweet tooth (I got one sweet, one savoury) this is a tasty pudding. Just like mother would make – if mother was a barmy old bat.

Ingredients

A sweet, rosy cheeked girl called Betty.
I've had some success with precious little
babes called Bethany or Buffy, but you
have to draw the line somewhere.

Some apples (optional, I never bother
myself) and some rabbit poo, which
gives the dish a little chewiness.

Lots of nits. Nits are so tiny that you
will need a magnifying glass, lots of
patience and a very, very small
knife to chop them. I have one
made out of a toenail clipping.

You don't need anything
special to make this recipe
— just a dash of love,
a pinch of sweetness,
and a great big child-
sized oven. Those nice
people at HaG make
a good one.

Method

1 This dish should be served hot with the eyes-cream melting into the crusty topping, so it's best to make the eyes-cream first, then it can get nicely cold while Betty is cooking. It couldn't be more simple to make; just whisk up Betty's eyes with some sugar, beaten egg whites and cream, then leave in the freezer for a couple of hours. You'll think I'm a big old silly, but I always think that brown eyes taste best.

2 Now you need to get the pudding in the oven. First slice Betty thinly, then grind her bones to make a fine flour. This can be a teensy bit messy so make sure you wear your second-best apron.

3 Take a deep pie dish. You need to make a layer of Betty, then a layer of apple, though I don't hold with eating fruit myself. You can get all the goodness you need from a nice young Cherie, and without the bothersome pips. Next add a layer of sugar, then sprinkle on a handful of rabbit poo, and start all over again with a new layer of Betty.

4 When there are about six layers mix up a dough made out of ground up bones, half a dozen eggs and sugar. I'm such a naughty girl that I still lick the bowl afterwards. Can you imagine? At my age! Spoon the dough over the top and sprinkle with more sugar and rabbit poo. Then into the oven with it for half an hour. If you're not careful the smell will make you dribble a little bit, so have a hanky handy.

5 To serve, put a nice big helping into
a bowl with a spoonful of the eyes-cream
and scatter with chopped
nits. A couple of chocolate
coated fingers poked into
the eyes-cream makes a nice
finishing touch.

Ingredients

Ten pounds of finely-powdered Fleur. The gingerbread needs to be light and moist so make sure Fleur is nice and skinny and throw her in a pond before you grind her into powder.

Ten legs, butter and sugar to taste.

Two firm young red-heads. You need to be careful when selecting your youngsters. If they're not ginger enough then you'll be left with a load of Auburnbread. Too ginger and you'll get an oven-full of carrot cake.

Classic Gingerbread

Ugla Snoganov

Eeee hee hee hee, hello deary would you like one of my lovely rosy apples? Oops, force of habit. I mean 'fa la la la la all the livelong day'. It's not easy being a beautiful fairytale princess at my age. All that dancing at balls and sleeping on peas does my poor old back no good at all. The only bit I don't mind is the kissing. I likes to whack a handsome prince over the head with one of my glass slippers, then wake him up with a big smacker from my sweet cherry lips. They all get sick when they opens their eyes and sees me leaning over them, but that's love at first sight for you. Butterflies in the tummy I expect. Mind you, it's funny that they all remember an urgent dragon that needs slaying right away. That dragon must have eaten about forty of my one true loves. Lucky for me I've got my toad, Prince William, back at the gingerbread house so I never need to go without a big slobbery kiss.

I don't do much witching these days, except the occasional spinning wheel, but I still like a nice bit of gingerbread after a hard night riding a pumpkin around. Made with ripe red-headed children, you can either eat it or use it as building material.

Method

1 First of all you need to catch your red-heads. There's always plenty sleeping under piles of leaves in the woods around my house. I just follow the trails of breadcrumbs until I find them, then drag them back by their ankles.

2 Light your oven and set to a medium temperature. If your children are called Hansel and Gretel be especially careful not to poke your head in while they are standing behind you. The mean little beggars got Old Mother Abysmal that way. It isn't right, cruel little children going around murdering poor defenceless old ladies.

3 Some witches like to fatten up the kiddies for a few weeks, but I can never wait. Get a large mixing bowl and beat them with a whisk until they are done in. Pour in the powdered Fleur, then break the legs and throw those in too, add the sugar.

4 You should now have a thick gingery dough. Pour this into long cake tins and pop them in the oven for about an hour. Although it's unlikely that the little darlings will push you in at this stage it's worth using a pair of long tongs and keeping well away from the oven door, just to make sure.

5 To serve, build the gingerbread into a small cottage, close by the huts of poor woodcutters who can't afford to feed their children. Use icing to join the loaves of gingerbread together, chocolate for roof tiles and garnish with lollipops and cakes.

6 One thing they never warn you about in the stories is the wasps, so make sure you have a can of spray handy. Before long the hungry local children should be swarming all over the place, giving you the chance to restock your larder. You might end up with the ingredients for Victoria Sponge, Pamcakes, and – if you find some very small children – Shortcake.

Whippersnapper Glory

Elvirissa Pursley

Uh huh huh. Good evening ladies and gentlemen, and welcome to Viva Las Vegas. It's a pleasure to be here with y'all on this very special evening of cooking and singing with the one and only me! Elvirissa! Uh huh. Tonight, I will be making Whippersnapper Glory, which is one of my all time favourite things to do with those cute, mouthwathering little babes. But before we begin cooking, let's start with a song, uh huh huh. You might remember this number two hit...

Love meat tender,
Love meat stew,
All my stomach fill.
Little children, I'll eat you,
Sizzling off the grill.

Oh, love meat tender,
Love meat raw,
Love meat in a tart.
Meat has made my life complete,
And also makes me fart.

Ingredients

If you've got a healthy appetite like me then you'll want a busload of whippersnappers in every shape and flavour. Each mouthful should be a Tutti Frutti taste explosion.

Eyes-cream (see the recipe on page 64. Nanny Todd's home made eyes-cream is just as good as mamma used to make.)

Whipped Karim for topping, plus a Cherie for the top and fireworks, flags, and umbrellas.

You'll also need the biggest sundae glass you ever did see.

Method

1 First you need to get ready to cook, it's important to be properly clothed. I find a studded leather jumpsuit with enormous sunglasses is very comfortable and practical. Any mess just wipes off. Not only that but you'll be pleasantly surprised by how sweaty and smelly it makes you. Once you're dressed, say uh huh huh to your audience and give them a song, something they can jive along to while you work, daddio. When I'm cooking in the diner I always like to start the show with 'A Whole Lotta Bakin' Goin' On'.

2 Snap your fingers and have your people bring the ingredients in. The first thing you'll need to make is the Dis-custard, so that it can get thick and cold in the fridge. It couldn't be easier to do, just hang a few spotty teenagers upside down and burst their pimples into a bowl, then add some sugar and stir like crazy.

3 Next, prepare your whippersnappers by chopping them into bite size portions and mixing them all up together. By now the joint should be jumpin' with crazy cats dancing by the jukebox and on the tables. Shake your hips and give them a few verses of 'You Taste Something Like a Hound Dog' while you grab a long, tall sundae glass. Now throw in a scoop of whippersnappers and pour on the Dis-custard, then add a layer of eyes-cream and repeat all the way to the top of the glass.

4 When the glass is full take Karim out of the fridge whip him and then shove him head first into a food mixer. This is a good moment to break into a chorus of 'Return to Blender'. Once your Whipped Karim is light and fluffy spoon him over the top of the Whippersnapper Glory and balance a Cherie on top.

Flat Jacks

Esmelia Sniff

When you're a busy witch who's spent all day chasing children through the forest, cooking in your restaurant and cursing customers what don't tip enough, it's good to put your feet up at the end of the day. There's nothing I like better than sitting in front of the fire with Tiddles in my lap and a nice piece of Flat Jack. Perfect with a hot cup of wee. This recipe is one of my best. Not only are Flat Jacks delicious, but making them is great fun. I haven't had such a good time since my rubber knickers burst.

You can make these lovely treats either crunchy or moist and chewy. Personally I likes them chewy, with bits that get stuck between whatever teeth you may have, and with a crispy bogie topping. A bit on the messy side to make, so make sure you wear an apron if you don't like getting your dress splattered. It don't bother me none. Just one Jack will go a long way if properly flattened, so you can take a boxful to a coven meeting and there will be plenty to go round.

Ingredients

A little boy called Jack. You can often find them tumbling down hills after fetching a bucket of water. If you're lucky Jill might come tumbling after, and it's worth sticking her in the larder, too. If you feel like something spicy you can make a nice Jilly con Carne.

Two pounds of freshly chopped bogies (crisp and crunchy or wet and chewy, whatever you prefer).

Two pints of honey. I like it with a few dead bees floating around in it.

You'll also need a steamroller (they can be borrowed from any good building site) as well as a shovel and a very sharp knife — every witch's best friend.

Method

1 Preset the oven to hot if you like your Flat Jacks a bit chewy, or very hot for crunchy, then takes your nasty young Jack from the larder. You want him nice and wriggly (it don't make no difference to the flavour, but I likes a good fight). Find a stretch of road and stake him out. Make sure he's well-tied.

2 Get behind the wheel of a steamroller, remembering to wear goggles – safety first. Run the steamroller back and forward over Jack until nice and flat, about one inch thick all over. It is traditional to cackle and mumble to yourself while you work, and I like to keep up the old ways. I even have a little song to mutter, what I made up. Talk about cackling, it makes me widdle meself.

> You're my next meal,
> Yes you're my next meal.
> Down there tied up prone,
> Flattened on the stone.
> By a rolling crone.

3 Scrape Jack off the road with a shovel and take him back to your cottage. He'll be too spread out to get in your oven in one go, so cut him up into neat sizes. Then put him in baking trays, pour on some honey and scatter with chopped bogies (for a crunchier topping pick off any damp snot still attached).

4 Poppet in the oven (arghh har har, geddit?) and bake for half an hour then remove from the baking tray and cut into fingers. Serve hot or cold.

The Poorli Belhi

STAFF WANTED

Do you have your own moustache? Due to an unfortunate squashing accident, the Poorli Belhi is seeking:

- 15 Handsome Waiters
- 1 Elephant Keeper

Are you the kind of person who likes to be motivated and part of a team? At the Poorli Belhi you will be thrashed along with all the other staff. We also offer poor rates of pay, long hours, and NO annual holiday allowance as well as all the elephant dung you can eat.

Janie Groviller

will be signing copies of her new book, which is much better than this one, at a bookshop near you soon. Queue early to avoid disappointment.

"More photos of Janie with no clothes on... Sigh."

★☆☆☆☆
Ivor Sickbag, *The Cackler*

THE BLACK PAGODA

YOU NOT WELCOME

Hungry?
Wanting GOOD time?

THEN GO SOME OTHER PLACE

Dishonourable Lady Soo-shi, she say. "You think I some kind of waitress? Eh, cheeky? You come to Black Pagoda I give you warm welcome over fire. You want magical evening? How about I curse you 'til bottom falls off and give Ping-Pong your eyeballs to play with, huh? How you like *that*?"

Shiela's Beach Hut

7–8 is unhappy hour!
1 cocktail for the price of 2

Shiela's Stinger
Lager with a deadly Portuguese Man o' War jellyfish floating on top. Shaken, not stirred!

Scorpio Rising
We trap a scorpion in a glass and irritate it with a splash of ice cold lager. Bottoms up!

Bruce's Octopus Surprise
A vicious, face-eating octopus squeezed into a glass with cold lager.

G.W.S
Great. White. Shark. A tall glass containing refreshing lager, a cocktail umbrella and nature's most successful predator. A cocktail with real bite!

Mad Elaine de la Moustache
Presents Fine Dining at

Le Shrug Café

Voted No.1 for unfriendly service, our motto is "You can't make an omlette without breaking legs."

2 Rue des Pouse
Toulouse

Elvirissa LIVE!

The Sweatiest Pits Tour

The enormous, the huge, the biggest star of Rock n' Roll in a Viva Las Vegas spectacular!

**ALL ELVIRISSA CAN EAT
ONLY $20**
This special ticket will entitle you to a special seven course meal, which Elvirissa will personally eat at your table before leaving you with a commemorative fart!

Iris O'Rambly's

Lucky Shamrock Tavern

Like Goblin, but too fat? Try our **NEW Elf Food** Menu

**Fairy Cakes
Frozen Boggart
Pixie Pasties
Crusty Trolls
Roasted Leprechaun
Brownies**

Live Irish music and dancing daily with Brendan Dooley, Lord of the Pants and his award-breaking band of Fiddlers! Mumblers! Leg wavers!

You'll be lucky to get out alive.

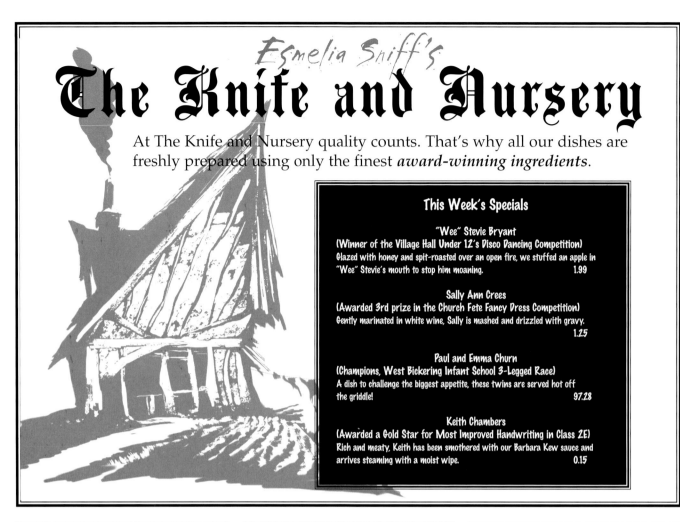

Esmelia Sniff's

The Knife and Nursery

At The Knife and Nursery quality counts. That's why all our dishes are freshly prepared using only the finest _award-winning ingredients_.

This Week's Specials

"Wee" Stevie Bryant
(Winner of the Village Hall Under 12's Disco Dancing Competition)
Glazed with honey and spit-roasted over an open fire, we stuffed an apple in "Wee" Stevie's mouth to stop him moaning.   1.99

Sally Ann Crees
(Awarded 3rd prize in the Church Fete Fancy Dress Competition)
Gently marinated in white wine, Sally is mashed and drizzled with gravy.
1.25

Paul and Emma Churn
(Champions, West Bickering Infant School 3-Legged Race)
A dish to challenge the biggest appetite, these twins are served hot off the griddle!   97.28

Keith Chambers
(Awarded a Gold Star for Most Improved Handwriting in Class 2E)
Rich and meaty, Keith has been smothered with our Barbara Kew sauce and arrives steaming with a moist wipe.   0.15

Gröanhilde von Warzhog's

The Sausage Zimmer

"Sausages made with our own Hans"

GOATHERD YODELLING EVERY FRIDAY NIGHT!*

*Followed by our speciality Yodelaayeehooo Sausage

Find us at the top of the
Whatsthematterhorn, Bavaria

Cabana Bedwetta

A Taste of Spain

Tweaking of the Bulls

Fiesta

Be trampled by craaaazy bulls!
Throwing up the donkey!
Dog Biting!
Lots of toilet!

Eat, drink, vomit 'til dawn to the sounds of Diego Lambada and the Tipsy Queens, playing hits from the movie "The Snowman", including no. 2 single "Walking in the Hair".

Special, surprise performance. The great Consuela del Diablo makes traditional Flamenco Dance with Chainsaws!

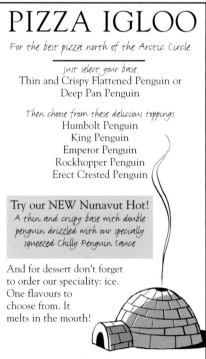

PIZZA IGLOO

For the best pizza north of the Arctic Circle

Just select your base
Thin and Crispy Flattened Penguin or
Deep Pan Penguin

Then choose from these delicious toppings
Humbolt Penguin
King Penguin
Emperor Penguin
Rockhopper Penguin
Erect Crested Penguin

Try our NEW Nunavut Hot!
A thin and crispy base with double penguin drizzled with our specially squeezed Chilly Penguin sauce

And for dessert don't forget to order our speciality: ice. One flavours to choose from. It melts in the mouth!

FREE delivery within 5,000 miles
CALL 0800 BRR RRR